Changing Matter

by Mary Miller

Chemical Changes

Two Types of Changes

Matter can go through physical and chemical changes. When a **physical change** occurs, the object still keeps its chemical makeup. A physical change can be a change in position, size, or shape. Other physical changes can alter an object's volume or phase of matter. For example, cut a log in half and it looks different physically. But both smaller pieces of the log are still made of wood.

Cutting a log results in a physical change rather than a chemical change.

A **chemical change** occurs when an object changes into a completely different type of matter. For example, if you toss the cut-up log into a campfire and it burns, the wood becomes a new material. It changes into ash and gas. These new materials have different chemical and physical properties than the log did.

Burning wood causes a chemical change to happen.

Evidence of Chemical Changes

During a chemical change, atoms are rearranged in a way that cannot be undone easily. They form different kinds of matter. A chemical change might show as a change in color. The formation of a gas or solid can also be evidence of a chemical change.

rusted horseshoe

Oxygen triggers many chemical reactions. When oxygen reacts with iron, rust forms. The gray metal turns reddish brown. The new color is evidence of the chemical change. A chemical change can also happen to a sliced apple. The sugars in the fruit react to oxygen in the air. The apple turns brown.

If vinegar is added to a bowl of baking soda, a lot of bubbles will form. These bubbles are carbon dioxide gas. Neither the vinegar nor the baking soda contains this gas. It is formed by a chemical change.

Rust can occur when metal is left outside for long periods of time. A chemical change causes the metal to change color.

Chemical Changes and Energy

Some chemical changes cause the bonds between atoms or molecules to break. Other chemical changes can form new bonds. The forming or breaking of bonds always involves energy. As materials react with each other, they either take in energy or give it off.

Some energy changes can be observed as they occur. For example, logs burning in a campfire undergo the chemical process of **combustion.** During combustion, the burning logs give off energy. The energy can be observed as the heat and light of the fire.

An apple turns brown when it is exposed to air.

A chemical change occurs when you mix baking soda with vinegar.

Types of Chemical Reactions

Chemical Equations

During a chemical reaction, one or more substances change into different substances. These new materials have different chemical and physical properties from the original materials. A substance used in a reaction is called a **reactant.** A reactant goes through a chemical change to form a new substance called a **product.** A product has a different arrangement of atoms than the reactant it comes from.

A **chemical equation** is a special kind of "sentence" that shows what happens during a chemical reaction. The reactants are written on the left side of the chemical equation. The products are written on the right side. An arrow is drawn from the reactants to the products. It works a bit like an equal sign in a math equation.

Mercury oxide is an orange powder. When it is heated, mercury oxide breaks down into its elements. These elements are mercury metal and oxygen gas. Heat is the energy source that breaks the bonds between the atoms of these elements. The chemical equation for this reaction is:

$$2HgO \longrightarrow 2Hg + O_2.$$

Mercury oxide is heated to form beads of mercury and oxygen gas.

Matter Is Conserved

Chemical reactions follow certain rules. One rule is that matter cannot be created or destroyed. Matter is only changed from one form into another. This rule is called the Law of the Conservation of Mass. It means that the total mass of the reactants must equal the total mass of the products. The mass you start with equals the mass you end up with.

For example, wood reacts with oxygen in the air to burn. The mass of the wood and the oxygen will equal the products of ash, smoke, and gases.

wood

When wood burns, no mass is lost. The mass of the wood plus the oxygen used is the same as the mass of the ash plus the smoke and gas released.

fire

ash

Three Kinds of Reactions

There are many kinds of chemical reactions. Sometimes, compounds split apart to form smaller compounds or elements. This kind of reaction is called a decomposition reaction. In this type of reaction, two elements separate from each other, just as one train car might unhitch from another. Remember the earlier example of mercury oxide being heated to form mercury metal and oxygen gas. That chemical reaction is an example of decomposition.

Other times, elements or compounds come together to form new compounds. This kind of reaction is called a combination reaction. To picture a combination reaction, think of one train car connecting with another. This kind of reaction occurs when zinc and sulfur are mixed together. They form a compound called zinc sulfide.

The elements in a compound can be thought of as the cars in a train. They can connect, disconnect, and switch positions.

A replacement reaction occurs when copper is placed in a silver nitrate solution.

copper wire tree

Copper is placed in a beaker containing silver nitrate.

Silver metal crystals form.

The third kind of reaction is called a replacement reaction. One or more compounds split apart, and the parts switch places. Think of two trains switching their cars.

An example is dipping a copper strip into a silver nitrate solution. The copper displaces the silver atoms. The products are copper nitrate and silver metal crystals. In some replacement reactions, two compounds switch places. For example, the compounds silver nitrate and sodium chloride can be combined. These compounds break apart and switch places. The new compounds formed are silver chloride and sodium nitrate. The sodium and silver switched places.

Uses of Chemical Properties

Separating Mixtures

Physical methods can separate substances in some mixtures. If corks and glass marbles are mixed together, they can be separated easily. This is because cork and glass have different physical properties. If you place the mixture in water, the marbles will sink and the corks will float to the surface.

A mixture of corks and marbles can be separated by placing it in water.

cork floats

marbles sink

A chemical reaction occurs when paint-stripping chemicals come into contact with paint.

Substances with different chemical properties can also be separated from each other. Paint can be removed from wood by using the different chemical properties of the two materials. Paint-stripping chemicals are specially made to dissolve paint. When they come in contact with paint, a chemical reaction occurs. The paint becomes soft, so it can easily be scraped off a surface. Wood is not affected by the chemicals. The paint can be removed without damaging the wood underneath.

Removing Metal from Ore

Ores are rocks from which we get metal. Ores are metals mixed with other elements. For example, zinc ore contains zinc oxide, a compound of zinc and oxygen. The zinc ore is heated in a hot furnace with solid carbon. The heat makes the oxygen separate from the zinc and attach to the carbon. The result is pure zinc and carbon dioxide. This process works because oxygen bonds more strongly to carbon than to zinc. This chemical property of oxygen allows people to separate zinc from zinc ore.

zinc ore

A smelting furnace separates zinc from the zinc ore.

When the colorless lead nitrate solution is added to a colorless solution of potassium iodide, a product of yellow lead iodide is formed.

lead nitrate solution

Yellow lead iodide forms.

flask containing potassium iodide

Chemical properties can also be used to separate elements from solutions. For example, lead can be taken out of a liquid solution. In this experiment, there are two clear liquids. The first liquid is a solution of lead nitrate. The second is a solution of potassium iodide. The solution of lead nitrate is poured into the solution of potassium iodide. As soon as the solutions mix, the lead reacts with the iodine. These two elements form a new compound. This new compound is called lead iodide. It is a yellow solid. The lead iodide can be filtered out of the liquid to remove the lead from the solution.

Identifying Substances

Scientists use physical properties to identify substances. Magnetism is an example of a physical property. Substances can also be identified by their chemical properties. Acids and bases are two common types of substances. Orange juice and soft drinks contain acids. Soap and ammonia contain bases. Strong acids or bases react more violently with materials than weak acids or bases do.

Lemons are acidic.

hydrochloric acid

vinegar

pure water

liquid soap

household cleaner

Soap contains bases.

Special paper is used to measure acids and bases.

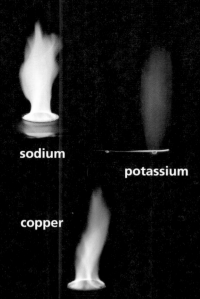

Metal	Flame color
barium	light green
calcium	brick red
copper	blue/green
lead	blue/white
manganese	violet
nickel	brown
potassium	lilac
sodium	yellow

sodium

potassium

copper

Acids and bases can be identified by their chemical properties. Acids and bases react with chemicals in a special kind of paper. This paper is called universal indicator paper. These reactions cause the paper's color to change. Strong acids turn the paper red. Strong bases turn the paper purple. Weaker acids or bases produce different colors.

Universal indicator paper is not used alone to identify a substance. Many different acids turn the paper red. And many different bases can turn the paper purple. The paper is a good start, but other tests must be performed to identify an acid or base correctly.

Scientists also use flame tests to identify substances. In a flame test, a material is heated to a high temperature by a flame. Different substances turn the flame different colors. For example, potassium turns the flame light purple. The flame color of the metal copper is bluish green. Scientists use special laboratory equipment to study the colors of the flames.

Uses of Chemical Technology

Health

Chemists have made important discoveries that have improved our lives in many ways. For example, many years ago, people often died from simple cuts. Bacteria infected the cut. The infection spread through the person's blood. There was no medicine to cure it. Often, the person died from the infection.

Alexander Fleming

In 1928 a British scientist made an accidental discovery. The scientist's name was Alexander Fleming. His discovery led to the creation of powerful medicines to treat infections. Fleming had been growing bacteria in special dishes. One of his dishes became contaminated with mold. Fleming saw that the bacteria near the mold died. The mold had produced a substance that killed the bacteria. Fleming called this substance penicillin, after the name of the mold. By the 1940s this chemical had become a lifesaving medicine. Today many medicines can kill bacteria. These medicines are called antibiotics.

penicillin mold

Fresh fruit and vegetables contain vitamins that help keep us healthy.

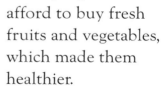

Years ago, some people suffered from a disease called scurvy. It made people pale and weak. Scientists discovered that if people ate certain foods, such as oranges and lemons, they would not become ill. Scientists identified chemicals called vitamins in these foods that prevented diseases. Today vitamins are added to many foods. Many people also take daily vitamin tablets. Diseases caused by lack of vitamins are now rare in the United States.

Fertilizers are chemicals that farmers add to the soil. These chemicals increase the amount of food that will grow. Nutrient-rich soil also helps plants grow stronger and healthier. In the 1900s chemists found ways to make large amounts of fertilizers in factories. Farmers used these fertilizers to grow more food than they had before. Larger harvests lowered the cost of many foods. More people could afford to buy fresh fruits and vegetables, which made them healthier.

Farmers use fertilizers to produce larger harvests of crops.

New Materials

Many materials used every day come from nature. For example, corn is a tasty vegetable. But it has many nonfood uses. Corn helps to make paper plates, makeup, and even crayons. Wood is a natural material used to make many things, including houses, paper, sports equipment, musical instruments, and furniture. But many common materials are not found in nature. They were invented by scientists. For example, the plastics used to make things such as toys, cups, and food containers are human-made materials.

In the 1800s scientists began trying to make a fiber to replace silk. Silk is soft and strong. It is a popular fabric for clothing. Silk comes from the cocoons of silkworms. The silk threads must be removed from each cocoon by hand. This difficult work makes silk very expensive. Early attempts by scientists to make silk were failures. Some human-made silks easily burst into flames. Others stretched out of shape. In the 1930s an American chemist had success. His silklike fabric was called nylon.

Natural silk is made from the cocoons of silkworms.

Nylon is a polymer. A **polymer** is a large molecule made of many identical smaller units connected together. In nylon each unit is made of six carbon atoms, seven hydrogen atoms, one nitrogen atom, and one oxygen atom. A polymer can have thousands or even millions of units in a single chain.

Plastics are another kind of polymer created by scientists. There are many different kinds of plastic. Many plastics are made with chemicals found in petroleum. Plastics are used in many everyday things. Some of them are very light and strong. Plastics are also inexpensive to make.

Nylon is drawn out as a thread from a beaker.

Transportation

Imagine riding a bicycle on a brick sidewalk. Now imagine that your bicycle's tires are made of wood. That would be a bumpy ride! Until the 1800s all wheels were made of wood or metal. Thanks to chemistry, our bikes, cars, buses, and even our shoes are more comfortable. It's all because of a material called rubber. Rubber has been around for a long time. It is a natural material that comes from plants. It is waterproof and flexible. But it melts in hot weather and becomes brittle in cold weather.

Rubber is made from a liquid collected from trees.

Bicycle tires are made of rubber.

Oil refineries separate the different compounds that make up petroleum.

In the 1800s chemists fixed these problems. By heating it and adding sulfur, the rubber became usable year-round. In the mid-1900s chemists discovered how to make artificial rubber.

In the United States many people get around in automobiles. These vehicles need fuel to run. Petroleum, or crude oil, fuels our transportation system. Petroleum is a mixture of many different compounds. These compounds are separated at large oil refineries.

Safety

Some chemicals have made life safer. The chemicals in disinfectants kill germs that can cause disease. Chemicals in medicines cure people of many illnesses.

For all the good chemicals have done, there are some dangers. If chemicals are used improperly, they can be hazardous. Manufacturers put warning labels on products that are dangerous to people, pets, or the environment.

household bleach

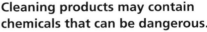

Cleaning products may contain chemicals that can be dangerous.

Warning labels are used to warn people if a product contains something that could be harmful.

medical waste

strong acid or base   harmful chemical

Many dangerous chemicals are found under your kitchen sink. The chemicals in cleaning supplies such as bleach, ammonia, and drain opener can be very dangerous. It is important to read the directions before using any of these products. The label might tell you to wear gloves or safety goggles. Many labels tell you to keep a window open for fresh air. Cleaners should never be mixed together. Mixing cleaners together can create dangerous chemical reactions.

Chemical changes are a big part of our everyday lives. They give us energy and special materials, and they even keep us healthy. In fact the book you are reading right now would not be here if it weren't for chemicals.

Glossary

chemical change   a change in which matter is changed into a completely different kind of matter

chemical equation   a way of writing what happens during a chemical reaction

combustion   a chemical reaction in which heat and light are given off

physical change   a change that does not alter the chemical composition of matter

polymer   a large molecule made of many identical smaller units connected together

product   a substance made during a chemical reaction

reactant   a substance used in a chemical reaction